Teresa

Echoes of the Tides

with love

Echoes of the Tides

Poems by

Adelina da Silva

To order additional copies of this book, contact:
Xlibris Corporation
1-888-795-4274
www.Xlibris.com
Orders@Xlibris.com
51266

Contents

Section Three

for my mother

My Race Began

Quando o descobridor chegou a primeira ilha
Nem homens nus
Nem mulheres nuas
Espreitando
Inocentes e medrosos
Detras da vegetação.
                    Jorge Barbosa

Yes, when the explorer came to the first island
There were no naked men or naked women
Watching innocently and fearfully
Behind the vegetation.

The tall ships with men holding canons
came from the north to the crescent islands
of rain with no ground to teal,
and no reason to remain
yet they conquered and placed their monuments.

The wild birds flew away,
the songbirds cried.
On parchment paper the explorers
would write a letter to *El-Rei*.

The islands stood naked; the sea
their only lover. The king with his dreams
of gold and spice a market
of men would set up
in Ribeira Grande.
Nigero-Senegalese, Sudanese,
Haussas, Minas and Bantus
would be bought and sent
as far as the Antilles.

In the islands, Jews, European
adventurers, refugees,
political exiles and African slaves
would settle.

$1+1 = 3$
They + them
Begot me
to inhabit the small
islands of futility
Cape Verde.

For 5 centuries the people would
cry their fate in *mornas*, song
rooted in Iberian nostalgia
and Islamic plagency,
protest and revolt in
Funana and Batuque
born out of slave chants.

On guitars, pipes, accordions
and flutes the islanders would
denounce famine, natives sold
to the *Roças of São Tomé*,
PIDE and tortured prisoners
in Tarrafal.

Later same sounds would be
heard in shouts of freedom in 1975.

Yes, when the explorers came
with ships, canons and promises to
El-Rei, little did they know—
—A new people and nation would be born.

Section One

Fogo

It's not my fault. Perhaps it's fate. I left.
Someone once told me that islanders are
like birds. They learn to fly away
from the nest very young. They return to die.

How many before me lie forgotten?
Nobody has stopped to place roses on
tombstones. For years I've been in search

of a port. Holding your photograph,
Fogo, my island. Every dawn is a challenge,
a freedom and a bondage.

I promise to return to you.
I'll come back to write you poems,
to play *cimboa* and violin on your beaches,
to dance in the rhythm of drums. To live.
Like the volcano, I'll chase away the old fate.
Ships will no longer take your children abroad.
But first let me tell you your story.

The House Near Alto de São Pedro

I liked mornings the best.
Dad went to work and mother sat
at her Singer, sewing.

The fish vendor came calling:
Atun frescu, quen cre? There was
always fresh tuna in the city.

No number, but the milk woman
came every day before seven.
No porch or driveway to speak of,

just a big *quintal* where Raul and I played
ball and rode imaginary horses.
Dad always stood at the dining room door

holding English toffees for my brother and me.
We'd stop our games and run inside to watch
for relatives who'd always come at lunchtime.

The clattering of pans, the warning whistling
of the coffee pot. Ah! The smell of *pexe fritu*
and the voice of *Tia Guta* calling us for *almoço*.

Now I live in Malden. My street name is Warren,
my house number is 30. Iva the milk woman died.
The family gathers at the table only

on weekends and holidays. Raul comes to visit
once a year, and I spend the rest of the days
remembering our childhood (not so long ago)

when we only knew of games and told
each other happy-ending stories.

The Pelourinho in Ribeira Grande, Santiago

Walking through the six towers of the Holocaust
Memorial near the Freedom Trail, Boston, I noticed
that some people read numbers, took pictures. Couples
whispered to one another while others passed
by in a hurry worrying about their daily chores.

I thought about the *Pelourinho*, The Whipping Post
in Ribeira Grande, Santiago, Cape Verde.
One summer afternoon I stood at the foot
of that monument watching children run
around, sing and play *roda*. Vendors sold
fried pork rinds, mangoes and *calabacera*.

I was twenty-three, knew little about my history.
In school they'd taught me about Portuguese kings
and queens, railroads and the Tagus River.
The *Pelourinho,* The Whipping Post,
was never a topic of discussion.

No names or numbers were written
on this Manueline style monument standing
in the middle of the ancient city many times sacked
by Drake and Cassard.

When I was eight and fifteen years old, I
walked by the whipping post many times
never knowing its white marble garment was
a mockery of purity, a symbol of royal abuse.

To some history becomes a memento.
Others learn stories of strangers and ancestors.
There'll be those to whom stories
will be just a passing of things, and those
who'll never fill in the blanks.

But on my walk in Boston on that hot June day,
I thought about the millions of African slaves, those
who stayed in *Ribeira Grande*, those who were
exported and whose stories were never told.
Does anyone hear them in the walls of sand?

Mulata

Offspring of a mixed cradle,
she lived with the sun and wind

wrapped in the waves and the sand
within the islands' bare rocks.

Maria Rosa, like many other *mulatas,*
woke up each day in her master's house.

She'd scramble to polish the silver, dust furniture.
At sunrise the ocean breeze would bring her hope.

Before sunset she'd find out that dreams
were not made for girls like her. Every night

she dreamed of her knight who'd one day come
to her rescue, but she'd been chosen to play a part

in her master's world. The sea's mistress,
the moon's confidant, neither magical

nor bewitched, a Woman. With the pestle
and drums, without riches or gold, her silhouette

no longer slender, her furrowed eyes mirrored her soul.
From her lips words turned into *mornas*

of despair. Her knight never came.
She raised her children at the mercy

of the ocean—her freedom or her bondage.
For years she watched her children grow up

calling their father, master. Years later
Maria Rosa would tell her son her story.

On his knees he promised to crown her queen.

The Fisherman's Fate

The moon's the fisherman's companion.
He carries his rod, his sandals,
a pound of eel for bait. Five hours
into believing in his patron saint,
still no fish come near. The sea
warns them there'll be a storm.

The fisherman shouts at the thunder,
San Pedro Santo nha fe,
Nho ten pena di mi—
Saint Peter, Saint of my devotion,
have mercy on me. The fisherman
holds tight to his rosary.
The whole island waits for him.

Early the next day, he comes to port.
He sounds his horn three times.
He's caught an albacore.
With their cameras, tourists
run to the dock. Restaurant owners
and rich families' maids will bet for the best
catch. The poor, last on the line,
will get the tails and bones.

The man ties his boat to the old mooring.
He thinks of the fish,
a hook fastened tight in its mouth
yet it didn't fight.
The fisherman's comfort will be the food
on the kitchen table and the smile
on his children's faces. His wife waits.
The wooden stove is not lit.

The Dry Season
Fogo, 1983

Seems like a long time
since the new moon came calling on us.

The Harmattan Wind huffs westward
packing pieces of Africa into a whirlpool

across the Atlantic. Saharan dust paints the sky
soupy yellow, air thickens, the desert threatens

to smother homes as the sun hides
in an orange-hazed—color overcoat.

December to March the wind stifles the soul
leaving a sea of sand that doesn't moisten.

Most flowers hide, but the *Senpri Noiva,*
pink and ivory, stand tall in the brown mist.

Immured between rocks and sea,
eyes fixed on the occluding sky, dimmed stars,

no planes or ships, no horizon,
my lips start to crack. I wait.

The new moon greets the island,
the sea and the sky embrace

and drive away the wind. I sit,
drink coconut milk beneath date trees

and dream of rain in June and the soothing
sound of hissing leaves.

The Candy Seller from Rua Serpa Pinto

*

I buy candies wholesale and charge one
scudu more to make profit.
Everyday I sit on the sidewalk curb
chanting: *Dos dropi pa sincu scudu.*

I try to convince the office workers
to buy sweets for their coffee break.
I chant. I hum. I chant some more
till someone drops five *scudu* for
two candy-bars.

The sun parades through the city streets,
the candy tray still almost full. Next
to the tray my baby sleeps. His bed
is a cardboard box.

The mercury nears one hundred. The streets
are under a red veil. The houses' windows shut.
Time for lunch and the afternoon siesta.
Nobody offers my child shelter, or gives me
a glass of water.
I hold a dish of rice made in rancid lard.
My baby sucks
milk and sweat from my breast.
My mind wanders into the past.
I hear mother chant at a sidewalk curb.
I am five. I am sitting on a stranger's doorstep.
Nhu cunpra dropis, mother cries. He walks away.

**

It's two p.m. The roar of jeeps wakes
the city again. Maybe the afternoon
will bring better luck.

The woman from across the street
walks down and buys four candies
and gives me twenty *scudu*.
Nha fica cu trocu. Keep the change, she says.

At 5 p.m. I get ready to leave. I wrap the child
on my back. The fan I bought at the *Loja Chines*
does not cool the heat or ease my troubles.
God, there is a Chinese store on every street.

In my cloth pocket a few coins clink
and a hymn echoes through the summer heat.
The woman across the street and I understand.
The Portuguese left and the Chinese came.
The poor pay for it all.

A Warning

The yellow rooster stands on the stone wall.
There was a time when, its comb held high,
its wings strong, brother took him
to the cockfights. Proud Madeira
always wore a crown. Sunrise, sunset,
it watched over the coop.
Sang.

Far away, another rooster's higher note
would answer. Head-lifted, stepping
forward, my yellow one would beat its wings
and sing an octave higher. Suddenly,
a second, third, fourth, fifth would fill the air
with their calls.

Now there is an empty coop.
The donkey hasn't seen a saddle for a year.
The well is dry, the cornfield a battleground
of grasshoppers. The yellow rooster stands
on the stone wall, its wings broken,
and feet tied with a nylon string.

My Childhood Days

To be a child again and run up
the hills of Bila Riba, my town.

There were no woods to go into
yet I hunted deer and lions.

Roses were few but my
garden filled with their beauty.

I climbed naked trees
and dreamed of vineyards and orange groves.

There were no rivers running to the sea
yet my ship in the stream's current traveled far.

Under the summer heat
I tasted trickles of morning dew.

I caught grasshoppers hoping that
they would turn into butterflies.

Rain was scarce. I lay in the mud,
and the puddle made a lake.

After the Drought

i

It is going to rain hard
as he closes the windows.
It's amazing how the elders
can predict these storms.
"Sta ben txobe riju"

ii

Children run
around the streets,
hold crosses made
of dead matches and twigs.
Lord have mercy, they sing.
"Miziricordia di Deus, Miziricordia."

iii

Now it doesn't rain much.
In the old days it would
rain for thirty days
and not let up.
The old man shrugs
his shoulders and tells
the children:
Gosi, ca sta txobe mas.
Txuba, e di bedju.

iv

In 1940 not a drop fell.
There was hunger in the islands,
war in Europe, no US dollars.
In 1942 they buried people alive:
"Do not bury me alive," many begged.
Ca nhos interran. N sta bibu.

v

Thump thump, thump.
Steady rain. Thunder rolls,
Mother gets her rosary and prays:
Santa Barbara Generosa,
Nha da-nu bida qui Nha vive,
Nha libra-nu di morti qui Nha morré.
My aunt and sisters repeat in unison:
Saint Barbara Generous Lady
grant us the life you lived,
but do not let us die the way you did.
Their murmuring prayers muffle
the hoofing sound of the rain
and wind and I run under
the gutters shouting, *Miziricordia.*

Mininu di Rua

The street kid's wrinkled T-shirt
would have smelled of dirt and goat's milk.
His torn, khaki pants didn't seem to bother him.
He stared at people
sitting in the city-street café,
their earnings displayed
in white wine and *Marmelada e Queijo*
crepes, the latest fad.

The street kid looked at posters of ice cream
hung on the restaurant windows:
butterscotch, rum raisin, butter
pecan. His eyes mirrored
the cheesecake, coconut and papaya flans.
His muddy face, his black fingernails
attracted only the flies.

Foreigners asked who he was.
The natives answered, *Mininu di rua,*
and the police shoved him away, saying,
Que fazer com o menino da rua?
What can we do with a street kid?

I remembered a day, thirty-seven years before,
when three boys snatched my bag of English toffee.
Then, we called them, *Mininu Mofinu,*
lower-class children.

The years have flown. We have changed
flags, presidents, but in the city all's the same.
The rich own hotels and cafes,
the workers join the unemployment lines,
a child still roams the streets.

Longing

She smelled like fresh green mango
picked in early June. She ran down
the rocky rivulets, her heart-shaped
face sticky with yellow juice. The wind
carried her voice to the high peaks
of the island's coconut and papaya trees.

The volcano slept behind clouds.
Thunder and lightning played hide and
seek with the sun. Streets turned into
rivers. The full moon rose over silver
water. Everywhere, earth smelled like corn
and cinnamon.

Oh, to be that child again and sing
under the gutters, *Miziricordia di Deus,*
as the rain poured on my head.

Now the wind has changed its direction.
The island is a desert. Crows fight over
garbage. Pigeons drink sewer water.
The trees are light posts in city streets.
Roses are covered with dust. The rain
fills them with one teardrop.

Do Not Cry for the Children

1

It's a hot July day in Santiago, Cape Verde.
As I drive to São Francisco, the roads
remind me of cinnamon
over a day-old dry sweet roll.
Es terra e quazi un dizertu.
This land is turning into a desert, the old man says.

2

Nhos vota pa mi. Mi qui ta tabadja pa nhos.
Vote for me. I am going to work for you,
the candidate for office calls, but the echo does
not reach the crowd.

The president waits in his suite. The inaugural
day for the new avenue nears. The prime minister
sends city officials with their metals tapes
to measure the roads. Soon there'll be water running.
But where are the pipes?

3

As the Trooper nears the small village, I see
children carrying water on their heads.
They walk two, three kilometers every day, I learn.
Cold imported bottled water sits on the tables in Congress.
The children turn their curious and friendly faces to us.

4

The parish priest feeds the children's souls during
Sunday masses. Between adorations and the rosaries,
he protests: Don't shed your tears when these innocent
faces are cold and the light of their eyes is dim.

5

Why does this take me back to my childhood?
I wore a red cotton dress and carried in my arms
an American doll. Then the roads, green aisles
that led to acres of banana and sugarcane and hills
of wild berries radiated under blue skies. Baby shrimp
swam in the streams that ran for miles.

6

The rain has left and with it the rivulets.
Sugarcane and bananas went with the
locusts. The harvest went with the west wind.
Others and I have left, and they still build the avenues.
The avenues, the newly built avenues, they'll
spread out and reach the coastline and many will leave.

7

The children. The children smile on the road.
There's nothing I can give them. They accept the answers
and hope for tomorrow.

Gethsemane

It's all they wait for, the dogs,
sunset in a cacophonous rhythm,
the nightly routine.
One barks, others reply, the songs
of revolt, some say.
There are strangers on the sidewalks
of Praia, Santiago, Cabo Verde.
The street lights are murky, stars flicker,
nothing on the horizon
but noise. The waves' rumbling
echoes in space. Pain? Agony?
Islanders don't cry. They fight
in the dry west wind.
The dogs bark. No one hears them
but I know that sound is the islanders' call,
the song of protest.
The *afortunados* now live in *Palmarejo,*
in villas made of basalt, with oak floors
and *Rozetti* tiles.
"Please take your *chinelu* off to step inside,"
their maids say. The once wide-open windows
are barred with iron.
Foreigners, immigrants, first ladies, ministers
walk by, their pockets full.
Trucks loaded with goods pass by *Praia-Plateau.*
Store shelves are stocked with foreign liquors,
Edam and Gouda cheeses, and canned goods.
People say, *Fidju terra ben libertanu.*
The maid's son stands on the Main Street
and watches. His T-shirt says in bold blue;
America. He dreams of Polo shirts and Levi's.
The dogs bark. Nobody breathes the same air.
He knows. He'll wait.

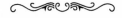

The Sound of Pilon

A

Pilon from *Guiné*
Mortar made of fig tree

corn, *Maiz* brought
by the Portuguese

after Columbus de *Cuba*
a España lo llevó?

B

Breakfast: *Sozinha*, a wooden pestle in her hands,
         pounds the corn for *cuscus*,

cone shaped, cake—
colored, glow
of sunrise.

C

Lunch: *Albertina* sets
         a wrought iron pan on her wooden stove

Djagasida cu congu verdi, xeren, rolon,
or scaldada served with roasted pork, fried
         sweet potatoes.

D

Dinner:
Time for *Catchupa*.
Corn with lima beans,

salted pig-feet and *tosinhu,*
cow's tongue and collard greens
served in a dish or china bowl,

E

Tenteren, camoca, brinhola
and *papabobra*. Ah, the smell
of corn and home-made butter.

Corn pounded, popped,
ground, kneaded, steamed,
roasted.

F

Corn in the *pilon,*
cutch, cutch
cutch

Sound of a distant past,
rain running down rivulets
into verdant valleys

and a harvest feast,
jogu di cuscus y asucar
game that my brother Raul always won.

G

Cutch, cutch
cutch

Fading
sound lost
in the drought

stolen by the West wind—
Mana of a Sub-Saharan land.

Bila Riba

The big house, my bookshelf of stories,
the long narrow streets,
my railroads of adventure,
the stories of the Wolf
that my father told me,
are behind the clouds, heavy
gray clouds.

Behind the clouds, Bila Riba
is my town: the volcano that kept me awake,
the moon that slept with the rising sun,
and those roosters
that awakened the island
to the ocean's sound.

The years, the color of the sun,
Mother sitting at her sewing machine,
a pink-laced cambric dress for my 7th birthday,
Christmas mornings and Easter Sundays—
—All behind the clouds, heavy
gray clouds.

Section Two

Chamada from America

Only twenty-one years old, Cousin Fina
couldn't accompany her family.
She didn't understand the INS rules.

Holding on to her family's promise
that she'd soon join them in America,
Fina sold her jewels and her furniture.

On her farm
she raised goats and sheep,
grew cabbage and turnips

near African violets and sunflowers,
sold chicken and piglets
to her loyal neighbors.

Fina postponed her wedding, anticipating
the letter from the US Embassy.
Every morning at her kitchen table

she'd cut collard greens for
her *guizadu* and sing her favorite
morna, Na Caminho di America.

Five, ten years passed, no mail came.
Her fiancé long-gone, Fina grew aloe
and marigolds instead. In a hoarse

voice she'd mumble the song of departure:
Partida e dor na nha petu, whoever invented
this pain knows nothing about love and suffering.

Fina died in her late forties. Her neighbors
always remember the day of her funeral,
an early November morning. On the way

to her grave the postman came running.
In his hands, a registered letter.

The Immigrant Road

1

We come from heat,
dirt roads, steep hills
to tar-covered highways,
to steel high rises, to snow,
sweet cotton-candy-like snow.

2

Suitcases full
of goat cheese, tuna cans.
Grogu Santo Antão
stains the white skirts
and leaves its aroma.

3

The rivers take
the place of the sea;
the roar of trucks,
the cricket chirps;
train whistles,
the roosters' calls.

4

The past dissolves
into this present farce,
no spectacle of brown.
I'd swear even the rocks
are wet in this town.

5

At Stop and Shop
mother cuddles pomegranates,
smells the quince, oranges
and inhales the scent.
I'd swear she thinks she's back home.

6

The body
has learned to dance
to a foreign tongue.
But the soul?

Echoes of the Tides

I sit on Clearwater Beach, America.
Cesária sings *Quen Mostrabu es Caminhu Longi,*
Who showed you such a far-away place?

People pass. I hear Spanish and English. Strangers
fill the cafés and bars. In the wind,
flowers dangle.

The tang of the sea takes me back to the island
of Sal. I wake up there on Santa Maria Beach.
The ocean sings of those forced into exile.

Women on the wharf sell tuna, lobsters.
Men unload their boats. Children chant,
welcoming me back.

I am home, but nobody knows me. I wait
to hear the ocean whisper why they forgot my love.
There's only silence.

I look at the sea, which is made of many sounds,
and the rhythm of drums. The tide echoes
in minor notes, *distinu di imigranti.*

The Saddest of All Sad Poems

"Puedo escribir los versos mas tristes esta noche"
Pablo Neruda

Nothing is written in the stars.
The ocean, the river, the hills,
nothing inspires me.
I've gone to farms. The shepherds
and their herds are simple creatures.
The muse isn't there.
I've read Pessoa, Giovanni, Cisneros
and wondered whom they call
when they hunger for words.
In a notebook, a gift from a friend,
I read: For the poet in you.
Once, I believed that I could write a poem.

Reading a verse by MacLeish—
"A poem should not mean but be"—
I recall a line of Neruda's
Puedo escribir los versos mas tristes esta noche.

Suddenly I answer: *Eu vou
escrever o mais triste de todos os tristes
poemas que tenho escrito.*
Yes, I'm going to write the saddest
of all sad poems I've ever written.

It will taste like pain, like a puncture
wound that never heals. Like long-lasting
grief and broken plans, unwritten notes,
the single rose you never gave me, a walk
we might have taken on Fonti Bila's black sand.

Yes, I can write the saddest of all sad poems—
a love poem.

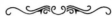

Nothing is the Same

1

The morning air brings a feathering
of goose bumps over my flesh, as I sit
on a bench in the city's park.
Nothing holds me. Nothing holds
me here. I want to go back to the summers
I left behind.

"All places are the same,"
my sister *Liche* says. "You make the changes."
A church bell rings. One o'clock.
Three hours ahead, across the ocean
the sun is hot and smells of the surf's tang.

2

All places aren't the same. I hear it playing
in my ears. The park, the sea, the sun,
the mountains, the black cat—all in memory's eyes.
Lovers lost in an enchantment. Their joy, my joy,
but I sit here. This city subsumes me. I am trapped

in promises of fame and luxury, blinded by the lights,
giant highways, and high-rises. I falter.
I dream of the black sands of *Praia Mosquito*.
Maybe when the rain streams downward
in warm sheets, it will be summer.

Mirror, My Companion

Summer's gone.
The breakfast table,
empty. Laughing

teenagers no longer
fight over scrambled eggs
and cold fries.

I move to the couch.
The baby no longer
jumps to my side.

The family photograph
tells me stories: Trips from
and to the airport,

picnics and gatherings.
Mama told me not to love
other people's children.

You should
have your
own

In the hall, I look into
the old mirror and hear
someone whisper

a sad lullaby.
There was always tomorrow.
I didn't listen.

The Poem I Will Never Write

I am writing this poem I said I'd never write.
I want to spit out the bitter taste in my mouth.

My fingers turn red then blue. I want to spill
the venom from my guts. I confess

that sometimes it pleases me to see you hurt
like I hurt. Let others know what you don't want

them to know. Your name doesn't matter. I can pretend
you're black, white, brown, a whole country.

I know. You'll say it's just a poem. You'll
think it's cool, or blame it on P.M.S. But

beware. There is a poem in my head.
It is no secret that I'm here sitting before

the white of this paper dressed in red.
Love? I do-not-know.
I'll stop and take pity on you and me.

I Stand Waiting

Midday
   sunlight
on the basalt
   pavement
—sweat on
   a runner's
forehead.

The heat on
   my front door-
step burns
   my feet.
A dining room
   clock ticks.
I, I look
   down
Artu San Pedro Square.
   A man walks,
Up—up—up
   the steps.
Brown hat—
   —a butterfly
jumping
   from flower
to flower.
He comes
   picks me up.
I am only five
   his tobacco
breath does not
   bother me.

I sit at the table,
    "Dad always brings me candy."
I cry.
    He pulls out
a chair
    smiles.
I reach to kiss
    him.
The room is cold
    and I am no longer
five.
    He's no longer here.

Pictures in a Curio

Dozens of photographs stand
on five triangular mirror
shelves inside a cherry curio
in the living room.

Father stands near an SUV.
His well-trimmed beard and
Rockport shoes signal pride
and his dream of America.
It's been six years since his passing.

Mother's eyes gleam. She's witnessed
her children's good jobs and one family home.
One wishes she'd smile more often.

Brother *João* has gone bald,
Brother *Raul* has put on extra pounds.
Lulula's (the oldest sibling) angry
lips hide her good heart.
João's sons, *Mario* and *Raul Alberto*,
are standing near a grill holding
their four children. *Raul's* children, *Mario
Augusto* and *Ivan*, are playing soccer with
younger brother *Uli* in the yard.
Oh! How I miss their summer visits.

Sister *Liche* is pointing her fingers,
giving orders, I am sure,
but we don't hear her through glass.

Three nieces stand in separate frames,
the two older ones hide their faces.
Suely, the youngest, has her hands
on a bag of candy, in her mouth an ice cream cone.

Like most photos these were taken
during happy family moments.
Years have passed. No new ones.

I clean the frames, polish
the days when we filled home with sun.
Each photo holds its own. Now we try
to keep the shelves from splintering.

Some flat, others glossy, the photos flash
the same family features in separate bodies.
Misleading portraits, perhaps.
They're standing on mirrors, after all.

A Girl Should,

pull down her skirt
cross her legs
comb her hair straight
play with dolls, not cars.

Mininu femea ca ta zubia
Mother used to say.

But I like to whistle,
I'd reply, but never
ask why. That was then.

Now I say, nonsense!

I refuse to keep face
playing the role of wife
while feeling like a whore.
No, to caring for children
who are not my own.

I'm neither the frivolous *Criola*
of our *coladeras*, nor the saint
and martyr men praise in our *mornas*.
I am not the made up doll
they've grown accustomed to.

I refuse to be like the others
who were molded to be "ideal women."
I refuse to open the door when
he comes home late with the smell
of whisky and another woman's perfume.
I've always been me, a simple
and candid woman.

Mother's Superstitions

Mother called out
    from the window
of the red Trooper,
    Passadinha si noba e sabi
canta otru bez.
    Do you really believe that
if the news is good,
    the bird will sing
twice? I asked her,
    as I switched from first
to second gear
    and maneuvered the steep
hills of *Achada Furna.*

E crensa di bedju,
    our elders' belief,
she told me.

No sign of turns,
    no guardrails,
but the red-beaked bird,
    would fly near
and sing.
    Mother was certain
our journey would be safe.

One summer
    in Spain
my friends sang
    old church songs
and murmured
    Hail Marys as we
approached every
    curva peligrosa
on the dangerous
    hills to Seville.

Through the window
    of a Renault 5,
    I found myself
—Surprise—searching
through the gray
    sky for a red-beaked
    passadinha.

Queen for a Day

*

The afternoon is warm.
In one of the village houses a young
woman sits knitting her trousseau.
She knits three days a week.
She's only eighteen,
a princess in her house,
her dad's favorite child.

Mother I'll be married at twenty-three.
Her mother does not complain. Her father's happy
to see his daughter in white on her wedding day.

In her husband's house, she'll soon reign,
the envy of her women friends: her house
fully furnished, silver-plated utensils, pans
and chinaware.

*

At thirty-nine her first child is sixteen.
She wakes up to clean, bake, cook
and iron the clothes. Sets the table
at sunset waiting for her husband
to come home.
He sits, eats and says nothing
about the dress she wore to complement
the dinner and leaves to return
at midnight expecting her to be
ready and meek.

Enough! I don't wait for
you anymore. I'm not afraid,
I don't make wishes. I don't cross
my fingers till they're blue.
I no longer hurt. I'm immune to you.
Now I set the table for one,
no red or white Mateus in the house,
no cologne, or cigarette smoke.

Was it you who smoked?

I haven't a clue.

She sits at her kitchen table
and relives a New Year's Eve
when she'd been the queen,
not forgetting that all year
another had been taking her place.

I put on my best evening gown
I stand and listen. Cars go by,
lovers walk hand in hand.
I wait for the one that stops.
They all walk like you.

Voices

She woke up. The room was dark,
her sheets soiled. The one-deciliter
of petroleum should have lasted
the night.

She looked around.
The cold walls stared back at her.

Mas un mininu, the mid-wife whispered.
Her husband had spoken of his conjugal rights,
the priest of commandments. The doctor
had recommended pills. The family planner
had talked of prevention.

She'd learned to obey rules. Nobody
asked her opinion. She knew she was
another victim of circumstance,
ignorant to some, naive to others.

In her mind her mother's words:
Deus qui da boca, ta da bocadu.
God would not forget the newborn.
He had provided for the other six.
Morning came. Someone handed
her the boy. Another gift.

Side Streets

1

The afternoon settles with diesel fumes
masking the smell of *caldo peixe* and *torresmo*
on the *Avenida Cidade de Lisboa, Praia*.
Five o'clock: People rush to bus stops,
the last *Hiaces* filled with vendors,
leave for the countryside in a plane of exhaust.

A warm rain begins to fall. The street sweepers
gather leftover newspapers. The clattering
of dishes, the murmuring voices announce
dinner and 8 p.m. Brazilian Novella.
A lonely woman stands under her umbrella
The moon *espreita* through silver clouds.

2

Morning awakes with the smell
of hot-brewed *Café di Fogo.*
From the neighbors' houses
doors bang, children rush
to the streets on their way
to school. Office workers wait
at the street corner, street vendors
put up their stands, *empregadas*
walk to *Pastelaria Montrond*
to get fresh bread and coconut cakes
for their employers' breakfasts.

3

Inside a brick house a man wakes up
to the eight strokes of the City Hall clock.
The empty space on the bed doesn't concern
him. He thinks she'll never leave him.
The sun creeps into his room. He knows little,
about anything, has no ties with the world
and the world knows nothing about him.

4

In search of what her friends call
the real world, she sees herself
in the glass of the bakery shop:
Why live without love, the promise of it.
And why let loneliness win?
Stand up and laugh at the world.

When Fall Meets Winter,

wild geese run
    wild on the cold
banks of the Charles,
    wooden ducks
look for a place
    to hide
and seagulls fly,

cold rain warns
    the autumn leaves
winter's near, find warmth
    I walk alone,
my feet cold.

Winds roar,
    snow paints the sky
white.
    Feeling the fury
of gods
    I run
and wait for morning.

I no longer fit
    in this scenery,
my home's a desert
    dry and lonely.

I dress in gold
    bathe in perfume
sleep under silk
    and brocade sheets
while you sleep
    on a bed of stones.
I lost my soul
    when we parted,
there are no ties
    to hold me back.

The Birds are Flying South

Looking up in the sky in mid-November,
I see flocks of birds fly away
from the city.

When someone first told me
that birds fly south
in the winter, I wanted

to hold on to their wings,
and see the world.
I knew they might not come back.

I had a few choice friends. They were
a part of my world. I loved them
but they left.

The sky darkens and night walks.
Solitude comes along while we travel
in different worlds.

And when summer arrives, new birds fly in.
I neither want to be sad remembering,
nor feel the pain of being in love.

Under The Eagle's Wings

1

Seventh in line
at J.F.K, Airport,
August 1990,
7:30 a.m.
No Threat Of Terror.
On my passport
an eagle soars.

2

8 a.m.
How long did you stay abroad?
What is your job?
The security officer asks.

3

I've been issued
traffic tickets
as Black, White and Hispanic
and paid different fines
depending on the neighborhood.

4

I have learned to play
the race game, checked
Black, Capeverdean
and Other for education
and job placement.

5

Even though I majored in English,
my last name grants me
translation services at hospitals
and other public offices.
I want to teach English.
My professor says,
Not here in the States.

6

My neighbor, a middle age
White male reminds me
in his daily talks
that I am not white.
You ain't black, says
my Afro-American friend.

Nobody bothers to ask what I think.

7

October 2001.
In the bus, public gardens,
and on churches' benches,
my complexion
poses a threat.
There's no shade of gray
in these United States.

8

Abroad, I hold
the American Flag,
aware of its consequences.
Here, I pay my dues
yet still carry the Alien Emblem.

Section Three

The Weekly Meeting

*

Three a.m. Thursdays, July 2004,
Logan Airport, the TACV Boeing
arrives from Cape Verde.
Crowds of teens in low-slung jeans
and Bob Marley T-shirts
push against the gate:
Hey, how you doing? Long time no see.
Good. Now N' sta in Brockteen.
Me, I'm still na Dorchester.

*

Nha Lila, a sixty-year-old woman,
has on her purple, pleated-polyester
skirt, a purse slung across her shoulder.
Her long, black braid protrudes from her yellow
silk headscarf. She walks through the crowd
exchanging hugs and kisses, and in a sonorous
voice lets everyone know her friend's aloofness:
Dulce, no hello? E sin que mundu! That's life.

A young couple fidgets a scrap
of paper looking for a familiar face.
A middle-aged man in his Pierre Cardin
suit meets his young bride while a teenage
girl argues with a friend on a cell phone.
The door to Customs opens. An officer sniffs
bags of roasted corn, homemade *marmelada,*
ponchi di cocu, sausage and *grogu Santo Antão.*

*

Observing this weekly ritual,
I stand against a pole
the way I always do.
Someone taps me on the shoulder.
It's Maria, my ex-student:
Hey Ms. How you've been? Still teaching?
Yes. How about you?
I am a hairdresser now. Here's my card.

Three-thirty a.m.
A middle-aged man comes out
of Customs, his hair and beard
dyed orange.
Hey, I call out to Maria:
El ca ba bu salão? He didn't go
to your salon, did he?

*

Newly arrived passengers and greeters
stand around talking: Some hand
business cards, some write phone numbers
and addresses, others promise to help:
*Cabu sta mau, no jobs, but N'ta trabadja
in a cleaning place. Bossa cren tcheu,
ca bu wory, N' ta help bo.*

Suitcases lay on the floor. Children
run around the long hall. A young woman
scowls as she drags her suitcase to the exit door
and hits a box. Cans of tuna, a bottle of homemade
butter, bottles of *grogu* drop out of the box.
A poignant smell of alcohol overcomes the crowd.
Darn! All that good brandy! an elderly man groans.

Outside the state police write
weekly tickets to the same
illegally parked cars.
See you next Thursday, a man
shouts to an officer.

*

A century ago we ran
down the wharves in New Bedford
and Fall River whenever the big ships
docked, unloading men to work
in the cranberry bogs
in Southern Massachusetts,
men carting dry yucca,
peixe seco and goats
to remind them of home.

Now we herd ourselves
to Logan in the middle of the night
hear the sounds of home, speak
Creolenglish.
We laugh at
the joke of life: we've made
a strange land our home.

The Man Who Came Looking For Riches in the 70s

i

A Capeverdean
came to Boston
came with a note
from a friend of a friend:
help him with room
and board until he finds a job
and settles down.

He arrived in snow
and frigid air
no smells of ocean
no familiar places
longed for sun
the tropical heat
Gentis rabés, ningen ta ri.
Strange people, nobody smiles.

ii

He walked to the Best Coat
Factory in Roxbury
looking for a job:
I not from here
spik liter Ingliss
my countré is in Africa
but I spik two lingua
come to find a job
in this bigga place.
My father say America rich

people make money
to live confortavel,
save, send to the familia
in ole countré.

I good working
I sent ticket
Minha mulher e filhos
not now, late
come to America,
good countré, I say.

iii

Ten years later
the man worked double
shifts, seven days a week,
slept three hours a night,
had time for nothing,
lived for his bank account.

I buy car
have money
for put down payment
in house, buy foorniture
refrigidera, everythin
for peopel, good life,
by now pay late
only America.

iv

Twenty years later,
My esposa come
childs go school
live happy my friend.
Maybe I go Cabo Verde
when I ole and ready to die.

Mudjer di Mercanu

His round-trip ticket in his pocket,
the old *Mercanu* had come back to visit his wife and children,
to buy an acre of land and a house for the family.
He'd bought them drums full of peculiar things
from the USA: perfumed soaps, powdered shampoo
and cologne.

He'd promised to write a petition,
filled in applications at the American Embassy,
left plenty of money in the bank, credit in the city's stores.
His two children did not cry.
He never stayed long enough for them to miss him.

His wife stood alone at the wharf and watched him go.
In 1901, when the schooner, *Flor de Cabo Verde*,
left *São Filipe* she had been twenty-two.
Saying good-bye for the first time had hurt.
Her man, in America, had joined in the whaling fishery,
then gone to work in the cranberry bogs.
She watched the years go by. Letters came and went.
Her grandchildren grew up.

Her husband never stayed when he came back.
"Marriage is a sacred sacrament," her mother told her.
Nobody had told her about the longing.

She saw her love perish. In the gray of her hair
her dreams. On her sixtieth birthday,
she was called to the American Embassy.
The petition had been finally approved.

She arrived on a winter's day in Boston, Massachusetts
and died ten years later. She told no one her story.
Many like her lie in graveyards
in Marion, Mattapoisett, Mattapan.

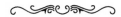

American, No Understand

I no understand
   when they talk
on the hand-phone
   on the train,
on the porch
   you hear everythin
about them
   and they mothar.
You know
   where I from
we no talk about
   our bisniss
to stringer.

They say
   you eata too much
sugar, too much salt
   I eat rice and beans
fish stew, bacalhau
   with olive oliu,
hot pepper and cumin.
   I no need buy
mechine do exercise
   I no need
nobody make
   me skinny.

They hear the drum
    Maka too much nose
they say,
    and I tell them,
I from the ole countré
    have hot blood
spik Ingliss good
    I dance *Funana*
no Rock & Roll.

They say
    You yella too much
They say
    Spik liter quite.
They tell me my job,
    I say
No you bisniss.

Everythin Hava Prizi

I come here in 1960
My brothar say to me
Five ears in America
I be cirizin.
You live na Europa
Twenty ears
No cirizin,
You childs born
No cirizin.
See, America good
My brothar tell me.

I be cirizin, I say him.
I go write documentu
I make testi.
I go my brothar, I say:
I too cirizin.
My brothar happy,
me happy too.

We go celebrashin.
My brothar say:
What they say you paypa.
I say, say about what?
You no, you collar,
You compleshin.
I don no, I say.

Me they put White, he say.
I look my paypa.
Sonababitcha
This peopel creizi.

You White, me Black.
We same mothar, same fathar
Why? They don no we no
White, no Black? We mix.

You no understand
in America you only
Black or White.
No Moreno, no Mulato,
my brothar tell me.

I go look job,
I get paypa. It say
everybody: White, Black,
Africa America, Spanish,
Indian. Some paypa say
Caboverdean, some
don say nothing. If I don put
nothin, they don give me job.
If I put Black they give me
job I don want.

My childs born here,
sing proud America Biutifool,
spik Ingliss, no Criolu.
If peopel shoot him in the stritu,
T.V. say: Caboverdean.
Next day newspaypa say,
maybe he no Caboverdean.
He do sunthin good,
nobody say what he is.
I no understand way
America work.
I thin when you cirizin
you be same like everybody.

English Learners

*

A funnel of words twist
through the page.
All immigrant children,
their eyes hungry, they digest
an English story.

Papers scatter off the desks.

*

Custodian, Mike scrapes gum
off the floor,

on his canvas bin
the phrase,

Toward a Better Future.

*

The immigrant children sit in class
listening to

Follow the Drinking Gourd,

the story of an old man
with a wooden leg who leads slaves north
to freedom.

*

These children don't learn nothing.
Mike says they've never lived so free.
The children must make connections.
There are so many questions: how the old man
managed his wooden leg, why he had
to come north, what if he had been caught?

*

On the classroom wall a painting
of men and women behind
a stagecoach reads:

"We Are Such Stuff as Dreams are Made On."

*

The teacher opens the grade book.
I wanna be like Shakespeare
José shouts.

*

Everybody respects the wooden-leg man.

Illegal Alien

1

Rosa lived in *Pico*
in a one-room hut
made of stone, covered
with papaya-tree leaves,
no water, no electricity.

In the coop, three chickens,
in the yard a pig, a stone grinder
for her *camoca*, a wooden
pilon for *catchupa,*
that is, if there'd been a good harvest
and corn on the island's farms.
Under her dry-leaf mattress
ten thousand *escudos*,
her ticket out of misery.

2

Rosa now lives in the basement
of a wooden house,
in a small town in southern
New England, works
two jobs for cash, buys food,
pays the rent and sends money
to her mama and her baby.

To fight the cold, Rosa lights
the stove, wears her wool coat
from the flea market. Her landlord
raises the rent. With no money
left and no green card, Rosa
moves from town to town
trying to find work
as she flees the INS.

3

Rosa listens to the radio and watches TV.
Her cousin was stopped near D.C.
with no papers; now he's a name on a list, a case.
Every night Rosa dreams of palm
branches heavy with dates. At sunrise she wakes
up to take on her daily battle,
ready for what might come next.

Everythin Diferenti

I look for job
    I marka apointmento.
I have garbega *na* my yarda
    I call the man, he say,
You have to make an appointment.
    Have pain *na* my back, tooth hurt,
cut my hair, need fix car,
    Everythin—
—marka apointmento.

I no kirin you,
    this countré stringe.
I don no, but I talk
    to my American frient-
—I think she my frient.
    I say, I go you house,
She say, you call frist.
    I call frist why, you not my frient?
Yes, but you call first
    and not after nine p.m.
I go home, I think,
    I say, she no my frient.

Yestday I say
    my frient from my countré
I go you house today,
    you belief she say,
call me frist.
    I tell you this no good,
Peopel come here, change.
    Now you see why.
You say I have no frient.

In my countré, frient
    you don say nothin.
You go knock at door
    and frient happy
to see you.
    Here, everythin is apointmento.
I tell you, I no marka
    apointmento to see
no frient.
I am stay in my house.

English as a Second Language

Tichar dixan fra-bu,
Let me tell you teacher, she says,
Nós minis, tcheu, dja perde ses mind,
Yes, many of our kids have lost their senses,
They smoke padjinha. Droga, you know,
That's trobla.
Drugs are trouble, yes, they are.

Before when we come to this countré,
everybody say, give job Caboverdean,
they good workin. Today, you know,
all diferenti. I tell my childs, go school.
You no study, you nobody, nada, nothin.
America is good, is bad. You choose, I say.
I work two job, help usband buy house,
pay car. No time take good care kids.
If I no pay atenshin, they go in the stritu,
learn bad thin.
I don no how you do? How you tich' em?

I tell them about me.
How it was hard to work and go to school,
learn English and make new friends, and
tell them to see where I am now.

They no lisin. If my boy give you trobla,
you slap his leg, push his ear.
In America teachers don't spank,
Ha! This problema with America,
or pull students' ears. It's against the law.
Law no good in this countré. You bit you child
you go jail. After you child bit you and people,
then they go jail.
I try tichar, but my mother never go see my
tichar when I go school. This countré tudo
diferenti, all taff. Obrigadu.

Yes, it is tough, but we come here
and work too much. *Nós minis,* our kids
are more important than *caza* and cars.
We need to take care of them *agora,* right now
not later, *asin mas tarde,* we won't be sorry.

Nhonho's Return

1962

Sixty-five years old,
Nhonho sits on his doorstep,
cane in hand.

Back to stay in Fogo, his native island,
he's bought a *sobrado*, a white folk's
house, and a grocery store.

Only seventeen he'd arrived in New Bedford
in 1914 on board of the Savoia,
become a citizen, fought for America

in World War II. After working for decades
in the cranberry bogs in Falmouth, Massachusetts,
he's come to spend his fortune.

In crates and *baús*: an iron bed, towels and sheets,
soaps, colognes, overalls and shirts, a Mussolini
hat and a gramophone.

Nhonho smokes Havana cigars, takes afternoon
walks with his Labrador. Now, even the upper class
ladies find him attractive.

Throughout the island some with admiration
praise the returned immigrant:
Americanu ten dola, ten dola sima burru.
They'd say the Americano has dollars.
He has dollars to burn.

Others with envy whisper:
Quen qui al fra, Nhonho moradu na sobradu.
Who would've thought, Nhonho living in a sobrado.

Going Back Home

When I return
to the Islands
let it be on a Sunday

when the cities are quietly
singing praises
to their patron saints.

When I return
to the Islands
a stranger amongst

my kin, I will
give back my love,
join in the psalms

and sing Hosannas in the gated
courtyard, call forth a big crowd:
churchgoers, children, beggars and drunks

for they will speak of their fate
and bring out the truth
as they see it.

When I return to the Islands
let those who hold
our destiny

in their hands be alert,
for the land will greet
its lost child

and together we'll eat,
feast and be free.

Traveling on a Not so High Way

Riding in a Mercedes on a tour of Santiago
I have an encounter with a dog that, mind you, chases me.

I step on the pedal, but the canine outruns the car
barking and scratching at the car window

showing that natural gas is better than petroleum.
I hit the brakes, the dog turns his back, lifts his left leg

and pees on my tires. I head on my way. I maneuver,
the curves, the hills, the rocks, the dirt, the chickens flying

across the road, the goats having their mid-morning
buffet on garbage left by the vendors' trucks

and pigs parading for my benefit. There is a traffic jam
far ahead. A pack of donkeys has decided to be asses

in the middle of the road. A kid screams,
E burru nhos sai di mei di strada. "You jackasses,

get off the road," as he whips the stubborn animals.
I stop to watch a herd of cows that join in the show,

I beep the horn, once, twice, and on the third beep
I swear a bull turns to me and in the bovine

language says: "I'll get off this road when I am done and ready."
I look around and I am the only 2-legged being. I turn

off the ignition, roll down the window, smile at the bull.
No one warned the animals that I was no stranger to this.

The Morning I Woke Up in America

October in Malden, frost on my windows.
Pumpkins and plastic ghosts rise from
the mound of orange and burgundy leaves
in my yard for children's Halloween.
Cartoons, Red Sox, and the Patriots on TV.
You're in America, they say.

Four dozen houses, three-dozen cars
on this inert street, in this flat town.
These neighbors don't mingle. They stand
alone deceiving, desolate, stripped
of common sense, buried in fear.

Three decades—Christmas Eve, 2001
in church, like every other Sunday
mornings thereafter we all sang
Alleluia and showed signs of peace.
For a moment fear was lost in songs of faith.
But it was only for a moment. In the church
parking lot we forgot the songs, and signs
of brotherhood were lost
in the fine threads of a dream.

Do I belong, a woman alone, trapped in a web
of futilities whose difference fascinates
some, enrages others?
If only they would strip the feathers
and look inside. They might question
my work, but I do not wet my tongue
in worship.

What is mine?
—Words. Yes, words.
No more songs of gratitude.
No more living for the dullest part
of my being. No more lying
beneath this veiled face. Their tongue
has become mine. I speak. Shout.
I write.